Kids on a Plane

Copyright © 2025 by Percy Comet

First Edition

First Published November 2025 by Rascal Books

All rights reserved. No part of this book may be reproduced, distributed, or transmitted in any form or by any means, or stored in a database or retrieval system, without the prior written permission of the copyright holder, except by a reviewer who may quote brief passages in a review.

ISBN-13: 978-1-9192330-9-3

ISBN-13: 978-1-9192330-8-6

All inquiries should be directed to:

Rascal Books: www.rascalbooks.com | info@rascalbooks.com

Percy Comet: www.percycomet.com

Written & illustrated by Percy Comet

Welcome aboard Kids!

Thank you for choosing Percy Comet Airlines.

Sit back, relax and enjoy the flight...

Their first time on an airplane, the kids were as excited as could be.

Lizzy and PJ waited for take-off with their hearts full of glee.

The airplane sped down the runway and soared into the sky!

'Something beginning with, C?'

Bored when the game had come to an end, PJ bounced on his chair and Lizzy pushed the buttons overhead!

They threw their socks and shoes into the air, and run along barefoot without a care.

The attendant looked on with shock and disbelief, and planned to put an end to all their mischief.

But before he could catch them, they reached the intercom, and suddenly without warning they burst into a song.

'Ladies and Gentlemen this is your 5 year old speaking!'

Lizzy poured soap down the toilet and filled the cabin with bubbles.

PJ left the tap running and covered the floor with puddles.

PJ swung like a monkey, from the bin overhead.

But it flew open without warning, and knocked the attendant on the head.

Now, Lizzy has the sun oil,

and over her head she pours it out.

The flight attendant finally catches her, but she slips from his grasp like trout.

The attendant was finally upon them, so they ducked under the seats and to make their escape they tunneled between the feet.

Lizzy led the way with PJ close behind.

'Look', whispered Lizzy, 'there's Mum and Dad's legs.'

Lizzy popped up like a prairie dog as Mum and Dad slept away.

Now the plane was getting ready to land,

but where was PJ?

The plane finally landed safely on the ground,

but where is little PJ? he is still nowhere to be found!

Mum and Dad are worried, where can he be?

"Don't worry," said Lizzy, "he is as happy as can be."

"Thank you for joining me with Lizzy and PJ on their airborne adventure! See you again soon for more fun and laughter!"

Your friend, Percy Comet

I believe in the power of laughter and imagination. A professional daydreamer and creator of funny children's picture books, I spend my days imagining wild and wacky adventures and then turn them into stories that make kids giggle!

Subscribe to my YouTube channel and website for lots of fun-filled adventures!

www.youtube.com/@PercyComet   www.percycomet.com

www.ingramcontent.com/pod-product-compliance
Lightning Source LLC
LaVergne TN
LVHW070434080526
838201LV00132B/269